# THE MINIATURE BOOK OF

# Valentines

## CRESCENT BOOKS
New York/Avenel, New Jersey

© Salamander Books Ltd., 1992
129-137 York Way, London N7 9LG, United Kingdom

This 1992 edition published by Crescent Books,
distributed by Outlet Book Company, Inc., a Random House Company,
40 Engelhard Avenue, Avenel, New Jersey NJ 07001, USA

**ISBN 0-517-08176-8**

Printed and bound in Belgium

87654321

CREDITS

Projects by: Juliet Bawden, June Budgen, Rosalind Burdett, Annette Claxton,
Gordon Grimsdale, Jan Hall, Suzie Major, Joanna Sheen,
Beverley Sutherland Smith, Sally Taylor.

EDITOR: *Sue Felstead*
DESIGNER: *Louise Bruce*
ILLUSTRATOR: *Pauline Bayne*
TYPESETTER: *SX Composing Ltd*
COLOUR SEPARATION: *Scantrans Pte Ltd, Singapore*
Printed in Belgium

# Contents

# Hearts Engaged

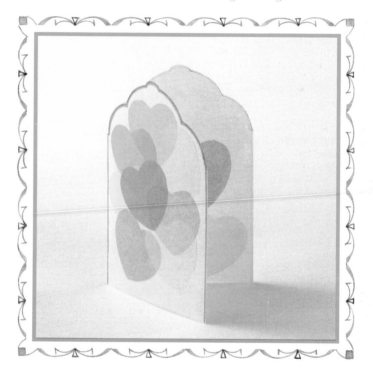

SEVERAL LAYERS OF PINK
TISSUE PAPER ARE USED TO
MAKE THIS PRETTY CARD

1 Cut card 22 by 16cm (8½ by 6¼in), score and fold 11cm (4¼in). Trace out the shape as shown and transfer to thin card adding 10cm (4in) to depth, to match card. Cut out and place on folded card. Draw round church window shape at top of card and cut through both thicknesses. Draw border with felt-tipped pen using a ruler to ensure a straight edge.

2 Place several layers of different shades of pink tissue-paper together in a pile on a cutting board. Cut out a heart shape template and use this to cut out approximately 10 heart shapes as shown.

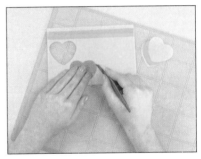

3 Spray glue hearts and position on card so that they overlap. You could stick more hearts inside card and also leave some loose so that they scatter when card is opened.

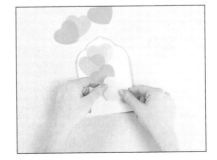

# Silk Valentine Card

PAINT PRETTY DESIGNS
ONTO SILK TO MAKE THIS
BEAUTIFUL CARD

1 If you really love someone, you'll want to send them a beautiful Valentine's Day card, hand-crafted by you. To make it easier, you can buy the card blanks in most craft shops or haberdashery departments. The designs here are painted on silk. Stretch a piece of white silk over a frame (available from craft shops) and outline the design with gold gutta.

2 Make sure the gutta lines are continuous so that the paint can't bleed through once the design is painted on. When the gutta is dry, apply the silk colours with a fine brush. Do not be over generous with the paint as the silk can only take so much before it is saturated and the colours start to bleed.

3 When the silk is dry, fix it according to the paint manufacturer's instructions. Then glue the silk in position on to the blank card and stick the mount down around it.

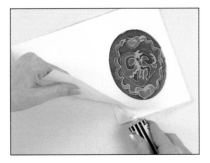

# Silk Flower Card

CHOOSE PRETTY LEAVES
AND PETALS TO MAKE THIS
ORIGINAL CARD

1 Collect together flowers and leaves of your choice and a plain greetings card – these can be bought from many craft shops and outlets.

2 Start by gluing the leaves in a curved design or a 'C' shape on the face of the card. This creates the basic shape of the floral display.

3 Trim away as much stalk as possible from the flowers so the card is not too bulky, then glue the flowers in position. Pearls or ribbons can be added in small loops to decorate the design, if wished.

# Paper Roses

THIS CARD USES OLD PAPER
BAGS OR WRAPPING PAPER TO
PLEASE YOUR VALENTINE

14

1 Cut card 20 by 30cm (8 by 12in). Score 15cm (6in) across and fold. With small scissors carefully cut out leaves and flowers from paper bags.

2 Cut wallpaper background, leaving small border of card showing. Mark a small dot at each corner with a sharp pencil, so you will easily be able to line up the background.

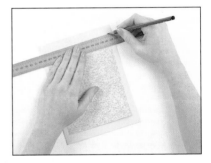

3 Spray glue on to background wallpaper and stick down on to card using pencil dots as a guide. Spray backs of roses and arrange. If you lay a clean sheet of paper over the card and smooth over the freshly glued pieces, the edges will not catch on your hands.

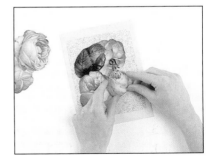

# Petal Valentine

GLUE DRIED FLOWER PETALS
TO A CARD FOR THIS
ROMANTIC VALENTINE CARD

1 Fold a thin piece of coloured card in half to make a card shape. Trace and cut out a heart shape from a piece of thin white card as shown.

2 Glue dried flower petals on to white heart working in rows from outside to centre. Use a rubber-based glue; tweezers will help to hold petals steady. Finish with a whole flower in centre of card as shown.

3 Cut border from a paper doiley. Spread a thin line of glue on outside of main card heart. Pleat doiley border onto glue all round heart. Stick petal heart over pleated doiley, cover with a piece of clean paper and smooth down. Hold for a minute until glue dries. Lastly stick on Victorian angel motif on top right-hand corner of card.

# Sweet-Heart

FILL THIS CARD WITH CAKE
SWEETS FOR A COLOURFUL
AND UNUSUAL GIFT

1 Cut a 3-fold card 42 by 19cm (16½ by 7½in), score and fold 14cm (5½in). Tape heart to back of tracing paper. Turn over and rub along edge of heart with soft pencil to make template. Line up heart tracing in centre of middle section of card and transfer outline. Very carefully cut out with a craft knife.

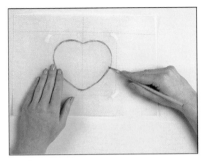

2 Place double-sided tape round heart aperture and around edges of left-hand portion of card, marked with a cross. Remove backing from tape around heart and place mould in position. Press to stick firmly. Put narrow line of double-sided tape around edge of heart.

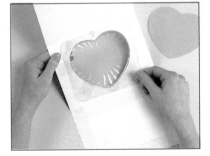

3 Pour sweets into heart until full and pack out with a piece of wadding (batting) cut to heart shape. Take off backing from tape around heart and from left-hand portion of card, fold over card and press down. A pretty pink bow is the finishing touch.

# Valentine Gift Box

GIVE YOUR VALENTINE THIS
ROMANTIC HEART CONTAINING
YOUR GIFT OF LOVE

1 Cut out two heart shapes from cardboard, one about 4cm (1½in) larger all round than the other. From red lining fabric, cut out a heart shape a little bigger than the larger heart. Take a gift box, wrap it in cotton wool (absorbent cotton) and place it on top of the smaller heart as shown opposite.

2 Cover the heart in the red lining, stretching it over the heart shape and sticking it firmly in position on the back with plenty of tape. You'll need to snip the fabric very carefully around the inverted point of the heart so that the fabric can open out to fit properly.

3 Cover the larger heart in white tissue paper, otherwise the brown surface may show through the lacey doily. Cut off a frill of about 5cm (2in) from the edge of four or five doilies, and pleat them up around the edge of the large heart, fixing them with tape. When the heart has been edged like this, apply glue to the middle and place the heart in position.

21

# Heart of Flowers

A BEAUTIFUL TRINKET BOX
WILL GIVE YOUR VALENTINE
A GIFT TO TREASURE

1 Cut a heart-shaped piece of ivory silk to fit the lid. Now cut 75mm (3in) of 6mm (¼in) wide ivory satin ribbon. Fold the ribbon in half, trim each end and glue to a small geranium leaf. Fix this near the point of the heart as shown.

2 Fix another leaf on top of the fold in the ribbon and then add leaves alternately to the right and the left, building up a heart shaped outline. When the shape is complete, fix florets of cow parsley over the inner edge of the leaves.

3 Fill the centre of the heart with rich red verbena. Finally, fix a small ivory satin bow to the top of the heart as shown below and assemble the box lid according to the manufacturer's instructions.

# Découpage Frame

THIS PHOTO FRAME WILL
TAKE PRIDE OF PLACE
ON ANY DRESSING TABLE

1 Cut out a heart shape from a piece of paper. Using this as a template cut out two heart shapes from stiff card. Cut out another piece of card that will act as a support for the frame.

2 Cut a rectangle from the centre of one heart shape and trim the edges of the second to make it slightly smaller. Cut around the outline of the découpage motifs and begin sticking them onto the card frame, the larger motifs first, then the smaller shapes to overlap these. Allow the edges of some motifs to extend beyond the edge of the frame.

3 Cover the second heart and the support with floral-patterned wrapping paper, ensuring that the raw edges of the card are also covered. Assemble the photo frame using glue between the layers, securing the back support firmly. Allow the frame to dry completely. Brush a layer of varnish tinted with water-based ochre paint over the frame.

# Valentine Delights

TINY GIFT BOXES FILLED
WITH TREATS ARE A
VALENTINE DELIGHT

1 These red and black boxes contain chocolate hearts for a Valentine's Day dinner. For the smaller box, first paint a plain heart-shaped wooden box red. Use a fine-bristle artist's brush to add black dots all over the outside of the box.

2 Place one or more chocolates in the box, along with some red ribbons for padding. Tie the lid in place with thin black ribbon.

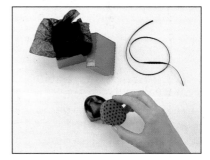

3 Add an individual touch to a plain red cardboard box by lining it with black tissue and tying black and white spotted ribbons around it.

# Heart Place Card

THESE HEART SHAPED PLACE
CARDS WILL GUIDE YOUR
GUEST TO THEIR SEAT

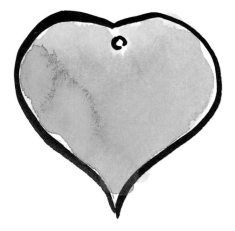

1 Heart-shaped place cards are perfect for a romantic dinner or Valentine's Day supper. Using the template above, trace heart shapes onto shiny red and plain white lightweight cardboard, and carefully cut them out.

2 Write the person's name on the white heart. Punch or cut a hole at the top of each heart, and thread a thin red ribbon through the hole. To add the finishing touches, tie the cutlery together with a wider ribbon, making a pretty bow. Then loosely tie the place cards to the bow, securing the cutlery as shown above.

# Heart Strings

THIS EASY-TO-MAKE MOBILE
WILL ADD FUN TO ANY
VALENTINE'S DAY PARTY

1 Cut out 40 hearts in thin pink cardboard and 40 in blue to the same size. Glue one side of a blue heart, lay the end of a long piece of nylon thread on it, and place a pink heart on top; press them firmly together. Continue this process with another two hearts, leaving a gap of about 4cm (1½in) between this and the first heart.

2 Add three more hearts to the thread. Cut off the thread about 20cm (8in) above the top heart. Make seven more heart strings. Cut two circles of cardboard. In one make eight tiny holes, about 2.5cm (1in) from the edge. Insert the strings and tape them in place. In the other circle insert four threads and tie them to a curtain ring. Glue the two circles together.

# Champagne & Roses

USE AN ICE BUCKET AS A
VASE FOR THIS BEAUTIFUL
VALENTINE ARRANGEMENT

1 Keep the champagne in the refrigerator and use the ice bucket for red roses! First, put soaked florists' foam at the base of the bucket. Then insert some variegated foliage – shown here is a spine-less form of holly. Intersperse this with eight or nine red roses, still in bud. Have two or three longer stems rising from the foliage to one side at the back.

2 Fill in all the available space with jonquil, following the outline. As you can see the gold is highlighted by the yellow-edged foliage. A handy tip: the roses will last longer if the stems are placed in boiling water for a minute before being given a long drink.

# Dipped Strawberries

EVERYBODY LOVES THESE –
DIP STRAWBERRIES INTO
CHOCOLATE AND RELAX!

**20 medium to large sized strawberries**
**60g (2 oz) plain (semisweet) chocolate, chopped**
**60g (2 oz) white chocolate, chopped**

Melt plain (semisweet) chocolate in a bowl or top of a double boiler set over a pan of simmering water. Stir until smooth.

Insert a cocktail stick into green hull and dip end of strawberry into chocolate. Place on a wire rack with the hull downwards to set.

Melt white chocolate in a bowl or top of a double boiler set over a pan of simmering water. Stir until smooth. Holding green hull, dip plain (semisweet) chocolate end of the strawberry in white chocolate, leaving some of dark chocolate showing. Place on a wire rack with hull upwards to set. Chill several hours.
*Makes 20 dipped strawberries.*

# Oysters with Caviar

THIS IS SURELY THE
TRADITIONAL FOOD OF LOVE
AND TASTES DELICIOUS

**36 oysters on the shell**
**2 tablespoons thick mayonnaise**
**or sour cream**
**salt and pepper**
**squeeze of lemon juice**
**1 teaspoon tomato paste**
**2 teaspons bottled horseradish**
**or to taste**
**3-4 tablespoons black caviar**
**fresh dill sprigs, to garnish**

Arrange oysters on serving dishes and sit them on ice.

Use a good mayonnaise. Season it with salt and pepper and stir in a squeeze of lemon juice and the tomato paste. Add the horseradish – the sauce should have a definite taste of horseradish so add more if necessary.

Spoon a little of this sauce on each oyster. Top with the caviar and garnish with a dill sprig. Alternatively, the sauce may be served in a separate bowl with the caviar alongside for spooning over the oysters.
*Makes 36.*

# Chocolate Truffles

SHARE A BOX OF CHOCOLATE
TRUFFLES WITH THE ONE YOU
LOVE ON VALENTINE'S DAY

**60g (2 oz/⅓ cup) sliced almonds**
**90g (3 oz/⅓ cup) sugar**
**750g (1½ lb) plain (semisweet or bitter-sweet) chocolate, chopped**
**1 tablespoon strong coffee**
**75g (2½ oz/⅓ cup) butter, softened**
**2 tablespoons whipping cream**
**2 liqueurs of your choice**
**cocoa powder**

In a pan cook almonds and sugar until dark brown. Pour onto an oiled plate, leave to harden. Crush to a powder.

Melt 250g (8 oz) chocolate in a bowl set over a pan of simmering water and stir in coffee; cool slightly. Beat in butter; stir in cream and crushed nuts. Divide mixture in half, flavour each half with 1 or 2 tablespoons of liqueur.

Gently roll heaped teaspoons of mixture into balls. Work quickly as chocolate sets fast. Set aside on greaseproof paper; refrigerate until firm. Melt remaining chocolate; dip some truffles and place on greaseproof paper to set. Roll others in cocoa when almost set. Place on greaseproof paper to dry, or place in sweet cases. Cover and keep cool.

*Makes about 1 kg (2 lb.)*

# Sugared Peel

MAKE THESE DELICIOUS
SWEETS TO ADD ZEST TO
YOUR VALENTINE'S DAY

**5 oranges, quartered, pulp and pith removed**
**600g (1¼ lb/3 cups) sugar**
**3 tablespoons golden (light corn) syrup**
**315ml (10 fl ozs/¼ cups) water**

Cut orange quarters (now just skins) into 1.5-cm (½-inch) strips. Cover peel with water, bring to boil, simmer 10 minutes and drain. Repeat twice. Bring 500g (17oz/2½ cups) sugar, syrup and water to a gradual boil, stirring. Cook for 20 minutes, without stirring. Add peel; simmer for 15 minutes, stirring.

Line 2 baking trays with greaseproof paper, and cover with remaining 100g (3 oz/½ cup) sugar. Using a fork, lift individual pieces of peel from pan and roll in sugar, coating peel well. Leave peel in single layer on baking trays overnight. Store in an airtight container, carefully separating each layer with wax paper.

*Makes about 250g (½lb.)*

41

# Almond Hearts

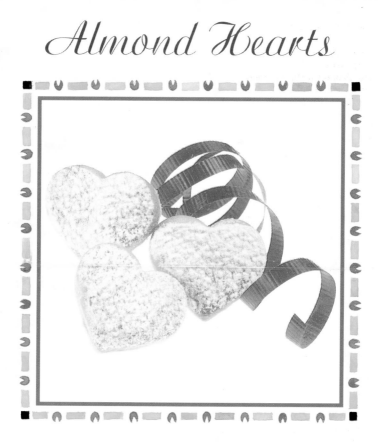

MAKE THESE CRUNCHY
SUGARED VALENTINE HEARTS
FOR YOUR LOVED ONE

**60g (2 oz/¼ cup) butter**
**60g (2 oz/⅓ cup) icing**
**(confectioners) sugar**
**1 egg yolk**
**few drops vanilla essence**
**90g (3 oz/⅔ cup) plain (all-**
**purpose) flour**
**1 tablespoon finely chopped**
**blanched almonds**
**To finish: icing (confectioners)**
**sugar**

In a medium bowl, cream butter
and sugar until fluffy. Add egg
yolk and vanilla; mix in flour.
Roast almonds in a dry
frying pan until light golden
brown, stirring; cool. Mix
almonds into sugar mixture
thoroughly. Form into a ball.
Chill if sticky.

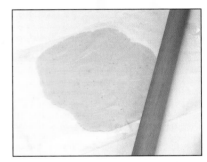

Preheat oven to 180C (350F/
Gas 4). Grease a baking sheet.
Roll pastry thinly between sheets
of greaseproof paper.

Cut dough into 80 hearts with
a small, floured heart cutter.
Place hearts on prepared baking
sheet. Bake in preheated oven 15
to 20 minutes or until a light
golden colour. Sift sugar over
hearts while still warm. Cool on
a wire rack. Store in an airtight
container with greaseproof
paper between each layer for up
to 10 days.
*Makes 80 hearts.*

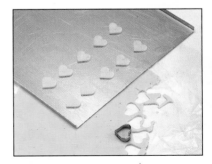

# Coeurs à la Crème

INSPIRATIONAL AND EXOTIC,
THIS DISH IS DELICIOUS AT
ANY TIME OF THE YEAR

**250g (8 oz/1 cup) ricotta or cottage cheese**
**30g (1 oz/5 teaspoon) caster (superfine) sugar**
**1 teaspoon lemon juice**
**315ml (10 fl oz/1¼ cups) double (thick) cream**
**2 egg whites**
**To serve: fresh fruit or bottled raspberry sauce**
**double (thick) or whipping cream**

Line 6-8 heart-shaped moulds with muslin. Press cheese through a sieve into a bowl. Stir in sugar and lemon juice.

In a separate bowl, whip cream until stiff. Stir into cheese mixture. Whisk egg whites until stiff, then fold into the cheese mixture.

Spoon into moulds, place on 2 plates and leave to drain overnight in the refrigerator. To serve, unmould onto individual plates and gently remove the muslin. Serve the hearts with fresh fruit with cream handed separately, or with whipped cream and raspberry sauce. *Serves 6-8.*